I0463220

Now Invest In Silver

An Introduction To Why Investing In Silver Makes
Sense

Andrew Henry

Now Invest In Silver

Copyright © 2010 by Andrew Henry

All rights reserved. No part of this book may be reproduced or transmitted in any form or by any means without written permission of the author.

The contents of this book are the opinions of the author and are not intended to be financial advice. The author makes no guarantee of earnings or profit and accepts no responsibility for actions or losses to the reader as the result of applying advice given in this book. You should always seek appropriate legal advice before speculating on investments.

Foreword

This book was written for of all those people who are currently feeling the financial squeeze of a recession and wondering if they'll ever get the opportunity to create true wealth for themselves and their family.

It's my honest opinion that learning about investing in silver is one of the biggest wealth-creation opportunities ever to be presented to the common man and woman on the street. The big problem is that because 'investing in precious metals' is a subject that would immediately turn off the average person with very little money to invest, the opportunity could very likely pass most people and never even get on their radar.

It is my true desire that this book bridge the gap between the educated and savvy investor and the everyday person on the street and enable anyone that reads to have a good idea of what the primary driving dynamics are that currently make silver the huge potential opportunity it is.

I am not a trader or investor by profession but feel it is my duty to do the best I can to ensure that this information comes to light and gets into the hands of those that most need it.

If the content is not technical enough for your personal tastes I apologize in advance for that and invite you to share the book with someone you care about for whom it may be just right.

Andy Henry

Table of Contents

Introduction 1

History 5

What Makes Silver Special 11

Why Silver Now? 15

What Type Of Silver To Buy 21

Coins Vs Collectibles 31

Buying Silver In Large or Small Sizes 33

Comparison Between Gold and Silver 35

Why Does Everyone Seem To Want Gold? 41

Wal-Mart In China 43

Where To Buy and Sell Silver 45

Conclusion 46

Internet Resources 49

Silver Terms and Acronyms 53

Introduction

For most people, the idea of investing in silver will sound as crazy as asking them to keep their savings stored as wood shavings. Investing is something that most people associate with trading and banking as opposed to something that 'normal people' do. This means that until an opportunity gets so big that it's on the evening news channel or mentioned in their newspaper, they're unlikely to know anything about it, let alone take the time to learn what's required to start taking action with an understanding of why.

In this book we're going to look at several aspects of silver and why it may now be something that people should take a look at seriously as an investment opportunity. We'll answer some common questions and highlight things that anyone can assess and draw their own conclusions about. There are also some common misconceptions about savings and investments which mean that people who are in the position to take advantage of the current situation may still not have considered something like silver because they've been given (or seen on tv) advice which never mentions this. A classic example is savings – how many times have you heard people say to put your savings in the form of ISAs or 410K etc. but never to invest in precious metals?

They're usually telling you this because those forms are tax free, but they also have a cap on how much you can save – you can usually do the same thing with silver but with no limit. A tax-free savings vehicle with no limit on how much you can put in – doesn't that sound like something people would tell you about? You'd think so – but they often know nothing about precious metals either and consider them as 'commodity trading' and won't have learned what you're about to learn about the special situations that make this so great.

As the reader you could have found this book in any number of ways and you could be living almost anywhere in the world, so while we will cover important information, specific things mentioned may not exist or may be called something different where you are. The aim of this book is to bring to your attention enough of the important information about this subject to put you in a position to come up with your own plan for your future. I advise you to seek out people in your area who are also knowledgeable and find local dealers and websites which cater specifically to your geographic location.

There are some great dealers around and as you will discover, having a great relationship with a supplier that can ship to you with low overheads or you can even visit in person will make your opportunity that much more effective. Paying for shipping costs and transaction fees and import taxes is one of the things that most investors just accept, but they're often an overhead you can avoid by finding a local supplier. The same goes for selling – why make your costs and the costs to your buyer higher than they need to be?

Silver can be a great investment. You can invest in it with only a few dollars or with more substantial amounts so there's really nothing to stop the average person from getting involved in what could possibly be the biggest wealth creation opportunity of their life. I have worked hard to make sure that the information in this book is straight-forward, easy to follow information which doesn't require any specialist knowledge. If you are serious about trading in large volumes you'll probably want to get hold of a specialist investing and trading book or advisor to focus your efforts even more and tap into some websites that offer live trading information and stock prices. I will focus on things that are important and necessary for you to know to be prepared to start from having known nothing previously.

One important thing to realize is the fact that silver can potentially be an even better investment than gold. People keep investing in gold because their profit margins are bigger. Just a little bit of gold can be worth $5,000, whereas a handful of silver will only go for a few hundred.

We will also cover some of the terminology that will be useful to you in your journey into silver investing and highlight some of the possible dangers from investing in coins and bullion. These things are very popular, but can be hazardous to an inexperienced investor. If you don't know what you're doing, you might end up spending much more on coins and other collectibles than necessary. Again, fear not, we will cover this so that your money should work for you and not against you.

Did you know that there is such thing as bad silver? If you don't know what you're buying, you might invest in silver that's less valuable than you think which of course is not good for you and your wallet, so we will talk about the differences between good and bad silver and how to use your money when investing.

Hopefully, you will be able to go out and start investing right away, but if you do have questions, feel free to contact me via the website at http://www.nowinvestinsilver.com

Even if you don't have any questions, feel free to send comments, suggestions or anything else you would like to share. I read my messages and e-mails personally and I will get back to you. I'm planning to create a readers spotlight section on the website and feature pictures sent in by readers when receiving their silver coins and bars and perhaps even interview you and share your story too, so don't be shy.

Anyway, let's get going with this, shall we?

History

If you've been able to take a step back from your busy life and look at what's going on in the world today you're probably in a state of shock. There are global cartels controlling everything from the media to the banks and most people are wandering around in a state of hypnosis that the governments are looking out for their interests and the media are representing their views.

The world is in bad shape right now in many ways and the financial system is just one of them. Many people have already written much about the manipulations that are going on all around us so I will try to avoid dipping into those issues as we go, but when you read about the state of the world's financial system I'm sure you'll wonder if some of the things I tell you are really true, after all – could the governments really let things get so bad? Well, I'm afraid the answer is yes and that's just the tip of the iceberg so rather than push you straight down the rabbit hole, I'll stick to how things relate to silver and why that's a good thing.

Some of what I share with you may be too much for you to accept from your current position, I felt the same way when I was first introduced to some of the things I now know to be truths of the way things are in our world. If you get the urge to burn this book because you think I'm crazy, just accept that I'm a normal guy who's just sharing some information and not trying to make you change your view, just hoping that your mind isn't closed to the possibility of things not quite being how you previously thought. I'm not going to go way out there on this as there are plenty of people you can find if you look around who will take you down the roads this information leads to.

Throughout the digital version of this book I'll use the opportunity to include links to various Youtube videos that demonstrate something I'm referring to. I urge you to read the book all the way through first and then go back and check out the videos. These are generally not my videos, but those of people who are sharing information I think you'll find useful. Including them in this book is not necessarily an endorsement of the person just a recommendation to check out the video. There are some good people with very informative Youtube channels though and I'll point you to them with a recommendation.

(If you haven't seen it, check out this Zeitgeist video – it's a great explanation of how we got to the current situation we're in.)
http://video.google.com/videoplay?docid=-594683847743189197#

I'm sure you're aware of the origins of today's money but we'll do a quick history lesson because it really comes to the core of the situation we're in today. Thousands of years ago when people were bartering items so that they could trade what they had for what they wanted, it had been discovered that there was a quite a lot more silver to be found in the earth than gold (around 10 times more), so while silver was precious, gold was seen as representing more value. People started to use silver as coinage first and then gold followed for more significant payments. This system worked pretty well, apart from the fact that you had to keep carrying gold everywhere in order to make the transactions. Not everyone wanted to have their gold stored in their home and so began the practice of storing peoples gold for them (for a small fee of course). These were the early banks as we know them today.

Fairly quickly people realized that just having a piece of paper that said they had gold in the bank was almost as good as actually having the gold and so the practice of trading using these pieces of paper or 'money' was adopted. At this point at any time you could take the note promising to pay the bearer to the bank and exchange it for the physical gold it represented. Coins were also minted that were made of gold and silver and represented that same value, but there reached a point where the material value of the coins weight in gold/silver became higher than its market value and so different metals and alloys were introduced and substituted in the minting process. So we see that a silver coin's face value does not always correspond to the true inherited value given by its purity and weight – in fact it could be higher or lower, depending on several criteria as we will see later.

It may surprise you to hear that many people still believe this is how money works today. The sad truth of the matter is that these days are long behind us and there is no amount of gold that could ever be swapped for the entire amount of money that now exists. In principle this is how things work, but in reality at some point between when banking began and recent times money was created for which there was no gold to represent it. (see the videos at the end of this chapter)

These 'fiat' currencies are the reason why you constantly see prices of the things you need to live constantly rising. Your fuel prices rising, your shopping rising and the explanation you're given on the news is always 'inflation' or some generic thing which just means "it's not something you can do anything about – it's the economy so just grin and bare it".

In actuality – banks are constantly printing more and more money to pay debts, pay for wars and things which they're saying get funded from your taxes. So – it's the value that YOU create that they're using. Every new dollar bill that they print from nowhere devalues the one in your pocket. They're stealing your money to pay for things which you often have no interest in paying for – but you don't get a say.

Actually, the banking system has gone way further than just this simple change and much of the world's value is now represented as debt rather than physical assets. The world now runs on debt and people have been trained to consider massive debt as the normal way of things. Newly married couples now tend to want their first home to be fully equipped with the latest modern conveniences and are happy to use debt to get it. If you borrow $10,000 from your bank, that debt is considered an asset and they are able to lend 10 times more than you borrowed based on it. In a way it's a little like when you join a gym – their facility may only support 50 members at any one time, but as long as you don't all go in at the same time – they can take money from 500 people and only need to supply 50 at a time. The money you owe the bank is used to lend other people and that money allows more to be borrowed.

I know this sounds crazy but if everyone who was owed money asked for it back today – there's not enough in existence to make the repayments. In fact, as I write this the American government owes so much debt that every family in America effectively owes $160,000. Of course, this seems ridiculous and you wouldn't imagine it possible but that's just one of the crazy things about the situation right now that you'll realize supports the position that silver makes a good investment.

Last year (2009) saw a massive financial collapse where lenders had been giving money to people who could never afford to pay it back – the end result was that government bail-outs were used to keep these lenders in business. Now, for most businesses irresponsible trading would result in bankruptcy and failure of the business and that should technically be what happened to these big institutes but because the economies of the world are so closely linked to them it was decided (by the politicians) to bail them out. The money used to bail them out has been coming from many places and is now part of the country's overall debt. At some level much of the money in circulation is tied to gold reserves as it was in the old days, but as part of the desperate measures to control the world's finances and stop the complete collapse of the banking system more notes have been printed and put into circulation. As with everything else – the more of something there is – the less each note is worth. The more money that gets printed to pay debts – the less valuable the currency is. We already know that there's more currency than supporting physical value in the form of gold, silver and other precious commodities, so where does this leave us? The answer is looking like being a crumbling US dollar and the need for a more stable way of representing value.

If you watch the news or the markets you'll see countries getting debts paid back to them in gold. China has been getting more and more interested in gold, telling its citizens to buy gold for their future and surpassed the US government in terms of gold purchasing. It seems Mr. Yi recognizes that (China's chief foreign exchange manager). He essentially said gold is too volatile, the historic returns aren't that great, and any gold buying by China would "certainly" increase Gold Prices and we know that silver will follow when these things happen.

There are occasional huge variations in silver prices and stocks when big investors like Warren Buffet take action (in 1996 Buffet bought 130 million ounces of silver and later sold it again), so silver prices can change dramatically if you're not paying attention. At the time of writing (March 2010) the current price of silver is at around $17.2 dollars an ounce. Of course this changes minute by minute throughout the day, so by the time you read this book it will definitely be different. I've made a point of creating a list of online resources for you so that you can get access to important data and information just by visiting my site and using it as the portal to get to everywhere else to do your silver research.

Now that we've looked at that little trip into history and realized that money isn't what it used to be, let's take a closer look at what makes silver special.

Some videos which explain this situation of a fiat currency now being in place where real money should be used are listed below – they do a great job of showing how the American dollar has evolved over the years and how history shows that the current problems were an entirely predictable consequence of moving to the Federal Reserve System.

http://www.youtube.com/watch?v=1FiaUpeJxcA

http://www.youtube.com/watch?v=FbyQB8e-rQg

http://www.youtube.com/watch?v=kM7rITeNW6U&feature=fvw

Even if you're not living in the US – Watch those videos, they're very short, very easy to watch and very good explanations of what's happened. I will also make them available at my website, so if you prefer, just drop by to http://www.nowinvestinsilver.com and you can find them there. They're by no means the full story but they cover the basics.

If you're reading the printed version of this book you may prefer to visit the website and just click on the links to those videos rather than type them web address in to your web browser as there are more links to come.

What Makes Silver Special

This is probably something you've never really noticed if you're not a silver bug but silver is actually a very special metal for lots of reasons. Some of them are to do with people's perceptions, it's rare nature and its historical place as part of peoples family assets (the 'family' silver was often seen as part of the value of a potential inheritance).

Probably the most significant property that will play a huge part in silvers value in the coming years is that there is no chemical element with higher electrical conductivity. That might sound like a boring fact on its own but it means that no matter what the situation regarding silvers normal perceived value, it has a property that means it is the 'best' metal for any application that involves carrying an electrical current. Think about that for just one second – There is no other metal on the planet that can do this job better than silver. That's HUGE. This means that no matter what happens in the future, using anything other than silver to conduct electricity is probably a compromise of some sort.

Now, if you've ever had to repair anything electronic or even metallic you've probably encountered something called solder. Solder is a metal strand with some flux (usually at the core of the solder wire but not necessarily) and it's used to melt around two metal contacts that you want to join together. Obviously silver is an ideal candidate to be used as solder, but for many applications the solder needs to be very soft and melt at low temperatures compared to the metals being joined, so lead and tin are most commonly used for 'soft' solder. For applications that need more strength and higher melting temperatures zinc and silver are commonly used.

Hopefully you're now starting to see why silver is not quite the same as gold for many reasons. Due to the small amounts of silver used in many of these electrical applications almost none of it is reclaimed or recycled. This means that when it's used in normal household appliances, cell phones, GPS systems, that silver is consumed and out of use for any future application. Imagine if that were gold, we'd probably have much more robust recycling methods in order not to lose that gold.

The other significant property of silver is that it is the metal with the highest thermal conductivity. This may not seem impactful at first glance, but consider our current global focus on energy conservation. Silver is not the only resource that we're raping our planet of and there are already many people focused on reducing the amount of resources we use in our daily lives and our travel. This thermal conductivity element of silver's unique properties is going to become ever more important to the way we address our energy conservation.

I'm sure you've heard of solar panels – what do you think would be the best element to use when creating something that needs to conduct heat and pass electrical current? Silver!

That's right – silver is going to be a critical material in the production of some of the newest and most in-demand products that our current world focus is pushing for. Do you think the batteries in the new 'green' cars will need silver?

Silver is already used in the windows of many large buildings because of its reflectivity. Silver is used in new ways every day and the things being created are the very same things that our global drive is aimed at making happen.

So, no matter what you may think about the ways in which old uses of silver may be reducing (photography could be one of those), there are more new ways to use silver being proposed than any reduction would ever equate to. It's possible that just one application of silver to be used in water purification purposes in the future would outweigh any drop from photographic uses reducing alone. On the photography point, there's also reason to believe that silver is an irreplaceable part of photography, even if just because no digital photography method has been produced that can store the images permanently. This might seem trivial, but do you really want to lose your lifetime of photos because the way you stored them was not permanent? I'm sure medical and military users won't accept that compromise. The current practice of storing digital photographs is to use memory sticks, disk drives and CDROMs. CDROMs actually use silver (remember its reflective property) and need replacing every 5 years to ensure contents are safe and you're probably aware of how temperamental disk drives and memory can be. These aren't the right answer and so you'll still see military and other important picture storage users reverting to the processes that involve silver in some way.

Because of its electrical and thermal conductivity, silver has grown in importance in modern industrial uses such as electronics in batteries where 1.2 million silver-zinc batteries are used worldwide each year; in solar energy as reflectors and conductors, making use of both its conductivity and reflectivity; in the automotive industry; photography, etc. Another important field is electro-technics where silver is used in conductors and commutators. The aeronautical and even aerospace industry use silver within a special alloy containing lithium and aluminum. Worldwide, silver is applied in more than 1,300 patents. As all of these things develop we'll see silver used in super-conductivity applications, health applications and electronics more and more.

I had considered listing all of the uses of silver I could find here for you, but I think you get the idea. New uses are coming out all the time and with silvers medical applications, thermal properties, electrical conductivity and uses as coinage and jewelry – there's no way we can remove it from consumption and we're almost certain to be constantly increasing the demand for the existing ways of using silver. You get the message now I'm sure.

On the market, silver is sold in different kinds of purity. The purest silver you're likely to come across, and the most popular investment grade silver is 99.99%, or 0.999 fine silver. Fine silver is the way silver is sold mostly in bars and some kind of coins.

Fine silver is too soft and easily deformed to create elaborate jewelry or any kind of silver objects such as cutlery or decorative objects. In these cases, different grades of alloys are used, one of the most common ones being the well-known 92.5 percent sterling silver.

As the grade of purity of sterling is 92.5 percent silver that means there's 7.5 percent other metals, usually copper, sterling silver can produce a certain reddish stain, known as the typical fire stain or fire scale, which is caused by oxidation of the copper.

Sooner or later the companies, the governments and other entities will run out of the silver they need. Today we demand more silver than we mine. Compared to the demand what we actually dig out of the ground is a very insignificant amount.

The majority of the current silver demand is fed by above ground stores and investment holdings and what comes from the ground is combined with that to try and supply our needs. Historically the above ground stores were significant but much of that has been used now by industry and coinage applications. My research indicates that in 1940 there were 2 billion ounces of above ground available gold reserves and 10 billion ounces of available silver – that was more than enough at that time. In 1980 there were 3.5 billion ounces of gold and 3.5 billion ounces of silver but the US government was flooding the market with 5-6 billion ounces of silver. In 1990 the silver reserves were depleted. Since that year we've been consuming silver at a higher rate than it's been mined. There are no government stashes of silver to flood the market with any longer.

In 2008 there were 5 billion ounces of gold and 1 billion ounces of silver. So the ratio of available silver to gold is constantly changing. It's been said that up to 95% of the previously existing silver has been consumed, unlike gold.

It's difficult to get accurate and up-to-date statistics on what's left in the ground, what's being mined and when we're likely to hit the point where things get critical.

All of these things ultimately mean that the price of silver is set to go up significantly for many reasons. If those things come together at the same time it's possible that the amount of silver that would currently buy you a suit could eventually buy you a house, and not in the too distant future.

Why Silver Now?

1-You're buying real money.

The main reason why silver is a great investment now is that you're buying real money. What this means is that you are able to buy silver, put it aside, and whenever you need money, you can draw from those resources and sell it in a day. In fact it is not uncommon for people to do that for purchases that require a lot of down payment. Let's say you want to buy a car. You are planning to pay a few thousand dollars down, but right before the sale is closed you find out that the down payment is going to be $1,000 or $2,000 more. Now, if you have that money in savings, that's fine, you can just take it out and make the payment as planned. If you don't have the money, chances are you're not going to be able to buy the car, unless you have something that you have invested in that you can sell quickly for cash.

That's why silver is so great. You can pretty much sell it in a day, no matter how much money you need. If you have the equivalent value in silver available, you are not going to have a hard time finding someone to buy it from you. You can put it aside and be able to use it when a crisis comes, or when you need big chunk of money quickly.

The great thing is that this investment will not be less valuable a year or two from now, as is the case with the dollar, for example. If you let your silver sit for a few years, there is virtually no way for you not to make money. If you buried a 10oz bar of silver now and dug it up in 20 years time it will very likely be worth in real terms significantly more than today. If you did the same to a $100 note – you'd be lucky if it was worth the paper it was printed on. There's no intrinsic value to a fiat currency and so a note can devalue to practically zero, whereas your silver bar will still be a valuable precious metal no matter when you dig it up with the chances being that the longer you leave it the less there will be around and the higher value yours will have.

2-You're buying something that's historically known

Silver was the first known coinage and was even mentioned in the bible (check out Genesis 1:28, Gen 2:12 and Lev 27:16, 2 Kings 7:1). People understand that silver is intrinsically valuable. This means that silver always was and always will be a good liquid investment. People will always attach value to silver, and in our times they will attach even more value to it because we use more of it every single day. Silver was always a metal that people considered valuable, and even though it is very cheap now, it will not stay that way. Silver is a precious metal and it will be more expensive as time goes by.

3-You're buying something that's negotiable worldwide

Let's say you have a lot of money on you and you go on a trip abroad. If you go to a country where they do not accept dollars as currency, you're going to have a hard time using this money. You're going to find it difficult to buy food, check into a hotel, or even pay for transportation. Simply, you will not be able to spend the money, or get the goods or services you need. That is not the case with silver. This metal is negotiable worldwide, which means that you can sell it anywhere in the world. There are people that invest in precious metals everywhere and as long as you have silver, you will be able to sell it in a short period of time and have cash in the local currency that you will be able to use right away. That is why precious metals are so incredibly important no matter what your circumstances are. Having something that you know you can turn into cash whenever you want is very reassuring as well as extremely important for the safety of you and your family.

I know that many people think that the dollar is an international currency and if you have cash, you will be okay. The problem is that this is not the case in many places around the world. I've traveled extensively for most of my life and I've made a point of always having something gold or silver available to me when in other countries so that I don't suddenly find myself with a wallet full of cash I can't use. I do have credit cards, but it only takes your bank or credit card company to put a 'security freeze' on your account because you're using it in a different country and you're stuffed until you can call them and confirm it's you trying to use it. This has happened to me so many times that I always have a backup source of funds now.

4-You're buying something that's in high demand.

As I mentioned before, silver is in great demand right now. We use it every single day to make electrical equipment, create computers, LCD screens, batteries and other supplies. Because of that demand, and because of the fact that it's very cheap now, investing in silver is a no brainer. I mean, you can buy silver for maybe $15 now. Because of the demand, in five or 10 years that silver you bought for a few dollars will be worth a lot more. That was the case with a famous writer named Robert Kiyosaki. He started investing in silver a long time ago and he bought it for $3 or $4 an ounce. If he was to sell it now, he would make about $14 profit on every single ounce he has now and that will keep increasing in the same way, which is why he says investing in silver will always be secure.

5-It's so cheap that people think it has no value.

I'm sure you realize it is very easy for people to get used to things and stop questioning reality. People tend to think that silver is so cheap that it just has to stay that way forever. We have many years of history showing that silver is significantly less valuable than gold. People are used to the fact that silver is cheap and they don't realize that the time will come when silver will return to its true value. The prices of precious metals always fluctuate, and if we watch those fluctuations, we can benefit from them and make money with them. The fact is that since 2005, which is just a few short years ago, the price of silver has skyrocketed. If you look at the charts, you will see that silver costs more and more every single year. For that reason if you invest in silver, you will be able to get a high return on your investment in just a few short years. Looking at the growth in silver prices we are seeing now; just imagine what it will be like years from now. We're approaching a tipping point at which the reality of the current and future situations will dawn on people. Once the message gets out that the currency which most people think is tied to real value gets so low that people stop accepting is as payment – things will get crazy and everyone will turn to truly valuable things to try to protect their wealth.

6-Not enough silver being mined.

Another reason why silver is great to invest in is the fact that new mines are few and far between. There is more silver in the earth to be mined, but the mining is not scaling up anywhere near as fast as demand is growing. This means that much of the silver that is mined is as a bi-product of other mining processes where a company mining for other materials sells off the silver it finds as it goes. When silver becomes even scarcer, which is happening all the time, it will be more valuable because people will still need it.

7-Silver reserves depleting.

Because silver mined is outstripped by increasing demand many reserves of silver are already very low or empty. Countries need silver for reasons already given, but because production is limited, we are slowly starting to run out. The US government has no silver left and has even turned to outside sources in order to be able to mint silver dollar coins. If you use this opportunity and invest in silver at today's prices, in a few years you will be able to liquidate it with a huge return on your investment. As time passes there will be less and less silver freely available and the price will go up as those that have it realize that it is in increasing demand. As I mentioned in the introduction to this book, it does not require a lot to invest in silver. You can start with just a couple dollars. If you have $30, you will be able to buy an ounce of silver; if you have $3000, you will buy 100 ounces. There is really nothing to stop you at this time.

8-Silver is consumed in industry more than ever before.

I think we've covered enough of that side of things for now and I'm sure you've got the message about the many and increasing uses for silver.

9-When currencies get weak people turn to precious metals.

There is a tendency whenever the economy is bad and currency loses its value for people to turn to precious metals such as gold and silver. It's close to impossible for silver to devalue over any significant period of time. People understand this, and that is precisely why they invest in silver when they feel that the value of their currency or any valuable currency in the world is dropping dramatically. When they fear an economic crisis, they go to silver and precious metal brokers and increase the bias of their portfolio towards safe value storage that precious metals offer.

That's a tendency displayed by every nation for many years. Use this knowledge for your own gain.

10-Silver price keeps increasing.

The last reason why silver is a great investment is that the price of silver keeps increasing. As I've mentioned before, silver is becoming more and more valuable and in just a few short years, it has doubled its market value. In 2005, it cost $7 to buy an ounce of silver. Now, it costs $17-$19 to buy an ounce of silver. The trend that you see here will not change. The price of silver will always increase, and the fluctuations will be minor within the overall context of silvers increasing scarcity and increasing demand.

The general tendency will be that gold will become more valuable and silver will follow but also have additional increases due to its unique additional uses. It is best for you to spend some money on gold and silver now so that you have a solid investment that you can realistically get back with significant increase in value in just a few years.

What Type Of Silver To Buy

There are a couple of things you can do to determine the quality of your silver.

1-Check the stamps.

Most of the companies providing silver to you will stamp or engrave the company name and silver content in the metal. Of course it is very easy to forge those stamps so that stamps alone are not enough for you to be 100 percent certain.

2-Certificates.

If a company is a reputable they will provide you with a certificate that will give you the actual weight of the silver and its purity to provide you with some kind of proof that what you're getting is actually good. Of course, those documents are very easy to falsify as well, so the fact that you have a certificate does not guarantee that you are not being duped.

The best thing you can do is to have a strategy when you purchase silver from someone new. The first thing is to buy a little bit of silver, literally just a couple of ounces, and then go and check it with a professional. Go to a professional that will tell you what the actual purity of the silver is, and if you are satisfied with what you find out, you can come back to your original seller and buy more from them. Obviously, at this point you don't want to fork out everything you have and just buy everything. Instead, buy a little more and check that batch as well. Just go back to your expert and check the purity of the silver again. This way you will make sure that you are not being given a different type of silver than what you have bought previously. After you are happy with what you have received, you can go back the third time and buy even more silver. This time you can be pretty sure that what you will get is a high-quality silver and feel confident spending more on that purchase.

'Junk-Silver'

The term junk silver is used by countries such as the United States, Canada, the United Kingdom and Australia to denote items that contain silver but are not necessarily up to the standard that an investor would seek. For example, your family silverware is probably not something an investor would be looking for, but nevertheless is valuable and is silver. The same applies to many old coins that have other metals in them.

Obviously, coins and other collectibles all are a little bit more expensive than just buying raw blocks of silver. That is because the sellers of those collectibles expect you to understand the value that comes from the fact that it's a coin, that it has a pattern on it, that it has been handmade, etc. They will ask you to pay for the fact that the coin is unique. If you are not interested in that, you'll be much better off, and it will be a much better decision financially to invest in regular silver.

On the other hand, if you don't have a huge amount of money to invest, and if you just want to kind of play around with the idea of buying and selling silver, then collectibles may be a good idea for you. This is a good start that will get you on the right track when it comes to dealing with silver. If you buy junk silver, you will not spend much money, and you'll still be able to learn from experience and practice what it takes to be successful when trading silver.

That knowledge alone makes it worthwhile to you to invest in junk silver so if you just have a couple hundred dollars to work with, then I encourage you to do this. If you're in the US then you may already come across a lot of junk silver every day in the coins you have when buying goods and services. Check the dates and start to keep any old silver coins minted prior to 1965. Today, you rarely see these pre-1965 U.S. 90% silver coins in circulation because although these coins are legal tender, their actual and true value is substantially higher than the coins' face value but since they are out there, keep your eyes open for them and you could start a silver collection with no actual investment capital.

As we know that there are different types of investors and different kinds of silver would meet their needs. Basically, there are two types of silver investments for the beginner to look into: The first and traditional one is to buy an amount of material silver which is sold in different shapes. The second, more abstract way, is buying shares, funds, accounts and certificates.

Material silver can be bought in bigger or smaller pieces, bars, coins, jewelry, in different states of purity, and even in abstract shares and funds. Let's take a look:

Bars:

According to standard, silver bars are made of 99.9 percent pure silver, or 0.999 fine silver. There are different sizes and weights, from less than one ounce (oz) up to 1000 oz. The most common sizes offered on the market are one kilogram, one ounce (31.1 g), ten ounces (311 g), and five grams. Silver bars are sold from specialized traders, or in some countries over bank counters.

Coins:

Coins can be bought either as original coins such as old U.S. half dollars, quarter dollars and dimes, which until 1964 were made of 90 percent silver, or 22.5 g silver per dollar. Many countries used silver coins in the first half of the last century. However, since the 1960's, minting silver into circulating "real money" coins isn't tenable for governments because of its significant increase in value during last century, so silver has been almost completely substituted by other alloys.

The second types of silver coins are the bullion coins minted out of 99.9 percent silver bars as a raw material. Different countries minted collectible silver coins in different years between 1988 and 2009: Canada, Mexico, China, America, Australia, Great Britain, Austria and Russia. The standard bullion coin weighs 1 ounce, with different degrees of purity, although there are some varieties of sizes available.

Apart from the governmental coin minting, there are also numerous privately minted silver coins, called rounds. It is common for these rounds to have a fixed weight of 1 ounce, and a purity of 99.9% and to be issued by different kind of companies all over the world.

This is something to look out for when you're starting out and looking around at what silver is a good buy for your first few times. If you're in the UK then the silver Britannia coin might be your preferred first choice, but you'll notice that Britannia's were not made from .999 silver, they're minted using .958 silver. This doesn't mean you shouldn't get them, but it's something to consider when you're looking at where to spend your money – if you can buy a .999 silver coin at the same price then obviously you would choose the other coin instead if your decision was purely based on the silver content. So be sure to spend the time to really look into what you're buying and how things are describe by sellers.

The great difference between coins and bars is that in order to determine the value of a silver coin, apart from its physical value given by weight and pureness there must be considered the numismatic or collector's value of a coin. Age, rareness, and provenance can determine the value of a silver coin just as much as its weight. So, the market value can be higher than the physical factors – an advantage which can easily turn into a problem because there are fewer buyers so it could be harder to sell and convert to money. Unless you're a coin expert or very knowledgeable about numismatics it's much safer to avoid getting involved in any purchases where the seller is trying to convince you that anything significantly higher than the standard spot price and other silver coin price is a good idea. There are a lot of multi-level marketing programs springing up and using silver coins as the 'product', but their appeal is for people who sign others up to overpay in order to get their coins cheaper – so please don't get suckered in to these things due to not knowing exactly what the situation is.

Jewelry:

Although jewelry is a very traditional way to buy silver, it is not really considered in the investment manner to which we're referring because we're looking for reference to the spot price for our calculations and jewelry does not align with that.

Certificates:

A certificate is a symbolic buy of silver without having to store the physical silver bar. The advantage clearly is that the buyer can purchase silver over larger distances without shipment of the silver bar. A certificate represents a certain amount of silver and its value depends on the actual silver value.

There are other things you can buy when you want to invest in silver, but these are the most well known and common and more than enough to get you started.

If you don't want to store the silver, you can buy it and sign a contract. This contract states how much silver you have, what the purity of the silver is and other important factors.

The problem is that the United States and other countries in the world don't necessarily have the physical silver to back those contracts. They don't have the actual metal. Although they are supposed to exchange those contracts for the silver, which you should always be able do because in fact it is your silver, they would not be able to provide you with the actual metal.

What does this mean? It means that if the investor pressed to get the silver that he owns, they would have to go and buy this amount from other people that own the metal physically. Of course, when your customer is so pressured, so desperate to buy, the prices are going to go up.

Imagine this situation: let's say you just bought a metric ton of silver. You have it somewhere stored in the bank, or another storage facility. You own it. It's not just a contract that you have signed, you were actually given the metal.

Now let us say that someone comes to you and says that they want to buy the silver from you. Now, if you know that the reason they want to buy it from you is that they are under pressure to fulfill a contract for the metal, you'll be able to ask almost any price you want.

That's why, silver being at $15-$17 an ounce right now, is such an amazing investment, and such a great opportunity. The United States government has had to stop minting some of its dollar coins because there is no silver to do it with.

I don't have to tell you what it means to someone who has it. I don't have to tell you how it changes the situation for them.

Now the whole thing I described may sound strange to you, and even a little shocking, but it's true. If you accept it and start investing in silver, you will always be secure because there is a constantly reducing amount of silver in the earth and there is less silver above the ground than is needed.

Silver Investment Tips.

1. Take a look at the market and spot price. (use www.kitco.com or similar)

Before you do anything else, you have to make sure that you know what's going on in the market. This doesn't only apply to silver. It also applies to other things like online marketing, off-line marketing, setting up our regular business, reselling anything, etc. If you know what's going on in the market, you will always stay on top of everything and you will never overpay for your product.

Find out who the reputable sellers are, find out who is good to work with, and take the time to learn who you should avoid.

Of course research is something you can do some of for free online. Just go to Google and look up anyone you come across, look up things you want to know about silver investments and check out the people, websites and Youtube channels I point you to. You will be presented with a lot of great results that will educate you in no time. It won't take long and it can really save you a lot of money and you can keep your finger on the pulse of what's happening with silver with the knowledge that you have experts to tap into online.

Always do the right research before doing anything else. Sit down at the Internet, spend a couple hours online researching, buy newspapers and read them thoroughly, or at least scan them to find information that is related to your silver investments, and most importantly find someone you can talk to that has the experience, and if possible try to find a mentor who will lead you along the way.

2. Educate yourself

Another thing you need to remember before you invest any money is to try to learn as much as you can, about macro and micro economic factors that affect such investments. Changes in these other factors are often massive signs that predict price changes. The historical evidence to support fiat currency collapses and extreme rises in the price of gold and silver are already there to back the current future of things, but you may also see more localized information that will give you new insights.

There are some very knowledgeable people running Youtube channels that are experts in this field and are accessible to you and happy to share their knowledge. Make sure you use that to your advantage and watch their videos, respond to their videos and ask them questions. Give them all the support you can so that they have reason to be there for you.

When you contact them, try to talk to them about what you want from them, being direct and honest with them. If they are nice, they will most likely want to help you somehow. If they don't have the time to help you out personally and talk to you, maybe you could pay for a consultation with them.

You are going to learn a lot from them, and more importantly you will be more equipped to start investing in silver safely and effectively. Some experts have subscription based services that give you access to their latest information as they create it, so that may also be an option you might prefer.

So I recommend you improve your education when it comes to investing in silver.

3. Find the right sellers.

Another thing that is important when you do not have much experience is finding the right sellers. The right seller will be the one that will sell you silver at spot plus a reasonable fee. Of course, you don't expect them to give you their silver for free, or to sell it to you at spot price, because if they did they wouldn't make any money.

You want everyone to be happy. You want your seller to make money, but you do not want him to rip you off. You want to pay a good price for your silver, so always do research before you decide to buy anything from anyone. Chances are that in your area or online there are many sellers that sell silver. Many of them don't actually sell their silver online because of high transaction fees, so be prepared to contact them and ask them any question you want, and based on feedback you can make a decision whether or not you're going to buy from them.

Never rush when it comes to investing your money. Remember that every dollar you're investing is hard earned money that you have to work to get, so don't throw it away foolishly. Take the time to get offers from different people, think things over and after you're done with that make a decision.

4. Start small.

Starting small is also something that is extremely important, or at least should be. Even if you have a lot of money available to you, you should never buy a lot of silver from someone you don't know. You should always start small. Buy a small amount of silver. If you feel that investment in silver is good for you after you have tried it, then go ahead and invest more money in it.

Go to the same person and buy more from them. Always remember, to check the quality of silver which you are getting. The best way to do it has been described, but I'm going to outline it briefly for you just so that you don't have to go back.

When you want to make sure that the silver and you are getting is of high quality, you should do a few things.

1. Buy a few ounces and check the quality of that.

2. If the quality is good, come back to the same seller and buy more.

3. Check the quality of your second purchase.

4. If the quality of that is good, come back to the seller again and buy even more silver from him.

5. Check the quality of that.

6. If everything is good, you are fine.

Remember that you can always sign a contract with your seller that will say something along the lines that if the silver is not of sufficient quality, you have the right to return it and get a full refund of the money you have to paid..

5. Keep your silver for at least five years.

Remember we have talked about how silver is supposed to become extinct in 2020. The US Geological Society said a few years ago that silver would be the first metal on the periodic table to become extinct and this could happen by 2020. This is of course just a prediction, but it does indicate that silver is becoming scarce. I know I have talked a lot about it, so I'm not going to go over it again, but I'm just going to remind you that the fact that silver is getting more and more scarce means that the prices are going to be getting higher and higher. In the past rhodium went from $3000 to $10000 almost overnight and most people in the public never even noticed, so don't expect those around you to be aware of this silver opportunity.

If you leave your silver and don't sell it for the first five years, you have a great chance of making a whole lot of money for not much work. Of course not touching your resources and not reselling your silver requires patience, but trust me, you're going to be glad you did. At some point we'll have to get better at recycling with the mindset that we currently have with gold. Ultimately silver will become more valuable than gold at the point where we've used so much of it that there is less silver than gold.

At the same time, you should always be on the lookout. If you see that the price of silver is beginning to skyrocket, you can think about selling before the five-year mark because maybe the rapid increase could be temporary. However, the general rule is, after you buy silver, let it sit for at least five years. If you want to, consider what your ideal exit price would be. Perhaps you're using the silver opportunity to pay for a car or home and you can work out exactly what the price needs to reach in order for you to cash out and achieve your goal.

Coins Vs Collectibles

In my opinion, buying silver collectibles is a waste of money. There are a few reasons why I feel that way, but the main one is, generally speaking, when you buy collectibles people want to get more money for the item as they are somewhat "prettier" and more unique than regular silver. The fact is that silver is a metal, and you don't need to store it in the form of coins, silverware, bars or any other item for it to be valuable. On top of that, collectibles are harder to sell than regular silver because you need to find a buyer who values its collectible nature and you have to demand higher prices to get a decent return on your investment.

You should instead focus on buying silver based on its purity and weight. Whenever you try to invest in silver, you should be presented with the "price per ounce" and you should be given information as to how pure the silver really is.

It is good to remember that pure silver (about 99.9% pure) is very difficult to handle as it easily bendable and it's impossible to make large objects with it. That is precisely why when people make collectibles they include a certain amount of copper or some other material to give the silver some strength and make it possible for them to create full works, spoons, and other items of everyday use.

Such mixing of materials will of course result in decreased value of the silver you are trying to sell. Remember, the more pure your silver is, the more money you can ask for it.

When you invest in silver, the percent and the weight are what matter. Of course the numbers minted on the coins indicate how old the coin is and when exactly it was minted, but it has very little significance to silver investors.

You might want to focus on this if you want to sell your coins to coin collectors, but silver investors don't care about the age of the coin at all.

What they do care about is as I mentioned the quality of silver as well as how much they're getting.

Obviously if you have a coin that's a really, really old, then you should think about what to do with it, but in general, the numbers that are minted on the coin don't really matter as far as a silver investment.

Buying Silver In Large or Small Sizes

This is one of the most common questions that people ask when thinking about investing in silver. There are two modes when it comes to buying and selling silver. You can work with small objects and then sell them as you go, or you can buy huge amounts of the precious metal in one piece and then sell it all at once.

Both of those models have their pros and cons, and it is mostly your own personal preference that matters when making that decision.

Generally speaking, it is easier to sell smaller items that are made of silver. There are people that have some money to invest in it, but they might not have enough to buy a big chunk of silver. If you have small pieces of silver, it will be easier for you to turn them into cash faster. At the same time major amounts of silver in one piece are usually cheaper per ounce than the smaller ones, which means you've got to be able to spend more on the precious metal and make more money with it in the long term.

Also to even turn this into cash you're going to have to look for investment companies that deal in precious metals which may not be very easy for you to do. At the same time if you are in the market and you know what is going on, you probably know where to go to buy and sell your silver.

It might be necessary for you to do some research before you make that decision, but when you get the silver bug, whether you have a big amount of silver no matter if it is all in one piece or in many different pieces, you will become knowledgeable about the market because it will become your life. Trading silver will become something you will do every day and you will want to know what's going on and where to go to buy and sell.

Let's consider some specific pros and cons when it comes to dealing with both large pieces of silver and small items.

If you buy a large block of silver, you will actually pay less per ounce than if you bought a lot of smaller items. But, on the other hand, if you want to buy a large amount of silver at once, you need to be prepared to spend a lot of money, whereas if you're buying smaller pieces of silver, you spend as much as you can, and then buy more later.

Of course if you have a huge chunk of silver, then when you decide to sell it, you will make much more profit. In fact, you might be able to get a few million dollars for it. The problem is, though, that you won't be able to sell that amount to an average person. You'll most likely have to seek out investment companies. On the other hand, selling small items is much easier because at the current rate, silver is affordable to pretty much anyone in small quantities. You can find many clients who will buy a small amount of silver from you and sell your silver off that way.

When you buy large amounts of silver at a discount, so will your prospects expect a discount when you try to sell it off to them. At the same time, if you decide to just sell off your small pieces of silver, then you don't have to apply discounts to it. It will take longer, but in the end you will have more cash in your hand. For some people the amount of effort involved in selling that much silver in small packets is not justified by the amount of money they make, and that's okay. It really depends on a personal decision.

Comparison Between Gold and Silver

The main difference between gold and silver is that gold is held by almost any country as a stabilization device for their currency. Therefore, gold has a special status; governments tend to keep the gold price stable or influence it by holding or selling deposits. Furthermore, gold is treated differently for taxation, being tax free in many countries. In the case of silver in some places the buyer has to pay taxes when purchasing silver – an amount that will be lost when selling. This has to be considered in profit calculations.

As we've already mentioned, the way that governments tax us and the various mechanisms for having tax-free savings may not have been as good an opportunity for investment as most financial advisors suggest and having a gold and silver portfolio alongside your ISA/401k might be a great consideration.

As gold is a good and reliable form of investment, and there is still a huge price difference between gold and silver, it could be questionable if silver really could become an efficient investment to return profit. Only one kilo of gold today is worth as much as about 50 kilos of silver. The key is in how much silver and gold will be available in the future, and therefore if increasing silver and gold prices could retain the same relationship as today.

The main difference in silver compared to gold is in the other uses that silver has. We've discussed them quite a bit now and those uses combined with the reduction in silver reserves and natural deposits make all the difference when looking at gold and silver.

In contrast, gold is hardly used for industrial purposes. National banks still hold large amounts of gold in order to control worldwide gold trade and gold pricing. In the case of silver, western governments have reduced their deposits so far they won't be able to have a major influence on price stability or development. During coming years, silver prices will mainly depend on the market laws of supply and demand. As we have seen, demand is increasing with the growing need of high end electronics and industrial products which contain silver and supply is reducing.

Silver charts of the last 10 years are showing a price progression from less than $6 to about $17, with peaks at about $21 in February 2008.

What factors determine the value of any good? Mainly, value is given by supply – the availability of a good - and demand. The more industrial branches need a raw material, the more precious it becomes as the amount of the available commodity gets smaller.

Gold is used in very few industrial products. The largest amount of gold is deposited in banks or bought as luxury items. Silver, on the other hand, is needed to guarantee our life standard and will become even more important in the near future. Silver mines will probably be exhausted within the next 15 to 20 years, so no new silver will be brought into circulation. For the first time in history, silver production in mines is decreasing – in a time of highest economic demand.

So why is gold still 50 times more expensive than silver? The real ratio of available gold to silver value is about 1:3 or even 1:5 – so actually, silver price should be 3 to 5 times higher than gold prices.

As gold is held by banks and governments in order to stabilize their currencies, they can influence the circulating amount and price. Gold circulation tends to be kept low to keep prices almost stable.

Silver, as we've learned, largely is not held in governmental deposits as money coverage, so price is almost totally regulated by the market.

Both silver and gold are very reliable attractive investments during a crisis. Silver, as the "little man's gold" is much more attainable for small investors. Not every investor is able to buy large amounts of gold. Silver can be bought by almost anybody. So, demand of silver coins and smaller bars will increase in times when people seek to save the value of their money. Both silver and gold save values in an inflationary process, so both are attractive in those times.

Although we're used to quite low silver prices, there have been historical silver peaks of about $806 dollars an ounce and gold price raised up to $2400 – a ratio of almost 1:3. The lowest gold price has been listed in the year 1919 at $20.70 an ounce. So it is not impossible at all that silver prices could explode with an increasing demand of industry, small investors looking for value, and new investors looking for the signs of the times. Considering the true available amount of silver compared to gold, it is possible and very likely that silver prices could overtake gold.

In the 18th century, the silver price ratio had been fixed to gold by many governments at that time, the ratio was 1:15, which meant one ounce of gold equals fifteen ounces of silver.

In the 20th century, gold prices increased far faster than silver prices, and the ratio became about 1:50.Since 2004 silver prices are rising constantly because of economic demand by industry and investors.

So obviously, today's price structure of gold and silver has not been historically stable nor can it expect to be in the future.

For the last 15 years, silver demand is above production. So far, governmental deposits have been feeding the lack, but are close to or already exhausted. Nowadays, countries are holding very little amounts of silver, and probably won't be able to balance the market for long.

Let's have a deeper look into recent silver demand:
In the year 2007, worldwide silver demand has been detailed as follows (Silverbook 2007):

ETF's (Exchange Traded Funds):	2,147t
Coins:	248t
Jewelry and Silverware:	8,801t
Industry:	25,561t

Industrial demand in detail:	
-Photography:	4,468t
-Electronics:	6,207t
-Alloys:	1,255t
-Catalysators:	1,501t
-Solar Energy:	980t

-Water Conditioning:	784t
-Batteries:	545t
-Mirror/ Reflection glass	495t
-Plasma Screens	330t
Food Hygiene	52t
Medicine:	49t
RFID Chips	47t
Stocks	16t
Chemical detoxification	16t
Wood Protection	15t

So we can see, the main demand is from industry; silver crafting, funds and the coin market together don't consume even half of the silver which industries use every year. As industrial branches like solar energy, electronics and other important silver consumers are increasing, demand will probably be even higher in the near future.

There are very many reasons why you should focus on silver and not on gold when it comes to investing in precious metals. In this chapter I'll talk to you more about that, and we will cover a few lessons that will hopefully explain to you why silver is a bargain right now and you should bias your investments towards silver and less gold. Obviously, if you have a chance to buy gold at a really good price, then go for it. We will not talk in this chapter about the exceptions where someone just gets a huge bargain in gold or digs up nuggets for free. Instead we will focus on general principles and rules that should be predictable.

More expensive.

The first reason why I think you should go for silver instead of gold is that gold is simply more expensive. Sure, your profit margin is going to be greater short term, but right now you will get a lot more silver for your money than gold and we've already suggested that silver is likely to overtake gold in value at some point probably during your lifetime.

Less scarce.

Scarcity creates value. Obviously, when there is not much of something available, what is available becomes more expensive. We are running low on the amount of silver and we have to use it every single day to create things we cannot live without so silver will become scarcer than gold and therefore more valuable. You probably already know that most of the gold that has historically been in circulation is still in circulation. This means that it is generally not used for anything except for making money and jewelry. Even though the profit margins from trading gold now are much higher than those you have when you trade silver, it is really a better, more long lasting and just a smarter investment to put money into silver.

Gold will always be there. We don't use it for anything expendable in our lives. Of course, we can have a gold filling, we can use gold in equipment, we can even use gold when making handmade suits, but these are all very luxurious, whereas silver is a necessity in many items. In other words a computer without silver will simply not function. You get my point.

So although gold can be a good investment it doesn't have the scarcity and investment 'potential' that silver has.

More people are starting to buy silver.

I know that when you invest a lot of money into something the reason that "everyone is doing it" might not be a strong enough reason for you. But that's not why I'm telling you that everyone is buying silver. The reason why I'm mentioning this is that as more people look around and realize the reality of the current situation they're starting to see this opportunity and buy silver now, and that means that the price of silver will go through the roof very dramatically and very quickly. Silver will become more and more wanted and people will just go crazier about it. Many of the big investment companies as well as wealthy individuals that people listen to, many thought leaders in the industry encourage people to go out and buy silver.

What do you think is going to happen if everyone starts buying silver? You are right, they're just going to increase the prices.

The great thing right now is that silver is really cheap, and you can get it at pretty much bargain prices. Silver is a precious metal and it will become expensive sooner or later. The thing is, the sooner you realize that, the sooner you're going to start investing in it and the sooner you'll be making money with it. Of course it is not my purpose to convince you to spend your money on silver, but I want to make sure that you understand the situation so that you can make an educated decision as to how to use your money most effectively.

Just like Robert Kiyosaki, who started buying silver when it was sold for $3 an ounce, you too can buy silver cheaply and sell it more expensively later.

Silver prices rise more rapidly than gold.

Another thing that's very important to realize when it comes to silver prices is that they grow more rapidly and more steadily than the price of gold. For instance, it was possible to buy an ounce of silver for $7 in 2005, now an ounce of silver costs anywhere between $17 and $18. That is the price for it right now. In just five years, silver increased its value by 100 percent. I am not aware of many opportunities to invest money that will return 100 percent profit after five years of basically doing nothing. Remember, that you don't have to work to increase the value of silver. All you have to do is buy when it's cheap, and sell in a few years.

Why Does Everyone Seem To Want Gold?

So we know that gold is currently much more valuable than silver. That's the general knowledge right now, and that's why companies that have money to invest prefer to buy gold over silver. Because they're buying and selling gold, their profit margins are larger.

Another reason companies invest in gold is that they know that gold is very popular. Over time, gold has always been considered one of the most valuable metals on this planet. People always traded gold. Kings wore gold all the time. Gold is used as a synonym of wealth. On the other hand silver is called "the gold of the poor", and of course none of the big and wealthy investment firms want to work with something that's associated with poor people. So, they select gold over silver.

But gold will decrease in value relative to silver because there will be much more of it as silver is depleted.

The main reason for which we use gold is to store value. Gold is our reserves. Gold is something that will be in demand and we will always be able to trade it for money or for anything we want. It will always be wanted and needed by almost any country in the world.

The crazy thing is that people don't really consider silver to be such a great way to store value. The reason for that is its price. If we want to have enough silver to even consider anything serious we have to have a lot of it. But as I have mentioned in the previous chapter it will not be a case for ever.

Silver will be just as good as gold as a means to store value in the very near future. We will want to buy silver from the investors because we will simply need it for our lives. This is common knowledge for many people that have interest in trading precious metals for long-term investments. Hopefully after reading this book this is common knowledge for you.

Wal-Mart In China

Now I'm going to talk about something that shocked me. I don't know if you're aware but there is a Wal-Mart in China. On the surface this doesn't mean much, but that piece of information got silver investors thinking and they calculated that if every man in China went to a super-market, be it a Wal-Mart or anything else, and bought a toaster and an iron, we would be looking at $50 per ounce of silver.

And that's only counting one toaster and a one iron for people in China. I'm not talking about the cell phones, or the TVs, the computers and other things they have. They use those things all the time and they will keep using them because the economy worldwide and the world in general has become so addicted to the Internet. The production of computers and other electrical devices will keep increasing from year to year.

China is currently beginning a massive economic boom which will bring a better standard of living to millions of people and as in the west will require production of more and more goods.

In fact, investors claim two years time from now silver will jump from $17 to about $40-$50 an ounce. And that's only in two years. Of course those things are just assumptions but this is a prognosis based on trends and on what's already happening around the market.

We also looked earlier at the recent Chinese focus on the value of gold and their focus on buying mining companies because they know if they spent their wealth on the physical gold and silver itself – they'd destabil-ize economies globally and massively increase the price of gold and silver. So while they understand the value of gold and silver they also under-stand the impact of massive changes in the dynamics driving the prices.

Where To Buy and Sell Silver

Once you're comfortable with what the current spot price is you'll be in a position to check out websites, online auctions, local dealers and other providers of silver.

Depending on your physical location there will be certain silver pieces which will naturally be more attractive. If you're in the US then the US silver dollar with the eagle on will probably be the easiest thing for you to get started with. If you're in Canada then the Maple leaf, in the UK the Brittania, Australia the kangaroo, Austria the philharmonic etc. The reason for having these preferences is not that any of these coins are more valuable than the other but that you are more likely to find a local source that means you don't have import taxes to pay just to take delivery of the silver. It's much easier to go to your local supplier and take the coins home than to have them flown across the world and wait weeks and pay import duties when they arrive.

Many people do buy and sell on Ebay, I even do this myself but because there are also dealers and suppliers who don't use Ebay due to their charges I have taken the initiative of setting up an auction site for silver sellers and made the fees much smaller. This is where I will be selling and buying much of my silver in the future as people find it and start to use it. This silver auction site is located at http://www.sellingyoursilver.com

Some popular companies you can find online are:

ATS Bullion

Baird & Co

Perth Mint

I've listed lots more on the website for this book.

Conclusion

We have talked a lot about silver. We have mentioned how it is becoming scarcer on the planet. We have talked about how it is becoming more and more valuable to investors like you and me. I've talked to you about how we need silver in almost any branch of our industry; how we need silver to communicate and even use the Internet.

Hopefully after reading this book you are not only excited about investing in silver, which was my main purpose, but you're also ready and prepared to start off. My goal was not to cover every single piece of information here in one book, but to help you realize the potential that silver investment has as well as teach you how to find the information that you need to succeed.

If you educate yourself so that you can make the right decisions at the right time, there is nothing that can stop you from becoming very wealthy.

Investing in precious metals, and in silver in particular, is one of the greatest business models I have come across in my life. This is about the only business model in which after you start you don't have to do anything to be successful with it.

After all, all you're doing is buying silver, letting it lay around somewhere and then selling it when the time is right.

It has been a pleasure to talk to you and I hope that we will stay in touch. You should always feel welcome to contact me and let me know how everything is going. I will try to be as helpful as I can and will always reply to your e-mail and letters.

The one thing I want to share with you before we part is that if you want to be successful with this business, you have to be focused.

Based on the fact that the price of silver will stay high and will be even higher year after year, we can safely say that silver is the cure for inflation. The dollar is plummeting, whereas precious metals such as gold and silver will go up and will always be more valuable.

What is more the price of the metal will increase so much that the monetary value of them will always overpower the inflation.

One of the most important things for people to realize is that even though real estate is really popular right now, there is something that's very particular about it that can cause it to decrease significantly in a short period of time.

Much of the current economic crisis was triggered by people being sold properties that they couldn't actually afford to pay for. The housing prices went up, people were tricked into thinking they could still afford them and sold policies which didn't kick-in to the true costs for 205 years. This was enough time for many of the lenders to pass those toxic debts on to other unsuspecting institutes but the bubble was always going to burst.

As we have become more and more buried in the financial and economic crisis we see more and more people don't have money to pay their rent or make mortgage payments. They will have to leave those buildings and those apartments and find something cheaper that they will actually be able to afford. A high percentage of Americans with jobs also qualify for government aid – people do not have a lot of money right now.

Now you probably know, what usually happens to a building that has been left empty. It becomes very hard to sell. That is why real estate, although it is a decent investment, does not give people the security that precious metals like gold and silver do. No matter what the economy is like, there is always going to be demand for silver.

Life without gold would be pretty much okay. We don't use gold in our everyday life in ways that we couldn't get by without, but silver is a completely different story. Without silver we would not have the technology that we have now. We would not have our cell phones, our computers and other things we use every day. We would not be able to use the Internet, to communicate with one another or even to make a cake for that matter.

Almost all of the pieces of equipment that we use each day would become extinct because for them to function they have to have silver in them.

Again, silver will always be in demand.

If people don't have money to buy an expensive house, they will not buy. If the economy stays as it is, they will not have the money for expensive real estate. They will simply not be able to afford it.

We can buy silver very cheaply, keep it around for a few years and sell it when it is in higher demand. Remember that as the Wall Street Journal expects silver is to be extinct by 2020. Now, the numbers might not be accurate, I mean, it might be 2025 it might be 2040, it does not matter. The fact it is that we are running out and we do not know what to do to get more.

Look at it this way, if the United States of America were able to get more silver, don't you think they would do it? It is not a pressing issue for them yet, but it will be, you just wait for it.

Internet Resources

I'll be making some videos showing how to shop around online and do some initial coin and bar purchases so look out for those at the website for this book http://www.nowinvestinsilver.com

Silver Youtube channels

http://www.youtube.com/user/nowinvestinsilver

This is my Youtube channel and I'll be uploading lots of videos talking about the various aspects of silver, showing you some of my silver as it comes to me and interviewing other people about silver investments. I'd love for you to share your videos with me and I'll give a shout out to everyone who sends me video responses.

I'll also be highlighting most of the following channels for you to check out but wanted to list them here for you to get started. There's some great viewing already in these peoples channels and many of them post regular video updates and can keep you very well informed about the dynamics affecting silver investments.

http://www.youtube.com/user/visionvictory

http://www.youtube.com/user/stellaconcepts

http://www.youtube.com/guildf40

http://www.youtube.com/user/TheBobChapmanChannel

http://www.youtube.com/user/manoftruth

http://www.youtube.com/user/JimRogersChannel

http://www.youtube.com/user/PreciousMetalsStore

http://www.youtube.com/user/backburnernews

http://www.youtube.com/user/endlessmountain

http://www.youtube.com/user/growby10

http://www.youtube.com/user/silverguru

http://www.youtube.com/user/marcchabotyt

http://www.youtube.com/user/maxkeisertv

http://www.youtube.com/user/myspacesecrets

http://www.youtube.com/user/schiffreport

http://www.youtube.com/bluecat1122

http://www.youtube.com/imitator777

http://www.youtube.com/inflationus

http://www.youtube.com/jberni1

http://www.youtube.com/kdenninger

http://www.youtube.com/davincij15

http://www.youtube.com/demcad

http://www.youtube.com/george4title

http://www.youtube.com/geraldcelentechannel

http://www.youtube.com/goldtothemoon

http://www.youtube.com/user/martysoffice

http://www.youtube.com/user/laroucheyouth

http://www.goldrush21.com/ - GATA

Last but not least here are a few websites to check out too.

http://www.nowinvestinsilver.com – That's the site that supports this book and that I'll use to provide supporting information and share all of these resources again.

http://www.kingworldnews.com/kingworldnews/Broadcast_Gold+/En tries/2010/3/6_Ted_Butler_on_the_Metals_Market.html

http://www.professorfekete.com/default.asp   Professor Antal E. Fekete is a renowned mathematician and monetary scientist

http://goldmoney.com/index.html - James Turk

http://www.goldsilver.com

Silver Terms and Acronyms

One of the hardest things a person getting into silver and coin investing has to face is learning the language that people on the market speak.

There are a lot of acronyms that may not be understandable for someone who's brand new. That is why I created a list for you that will get you through the first and most important abbreviations. Again, this list is by no means comprehensive and there are many more things that should be added to it, but I did not want to overwhelm you with the amount of information.

What you have before you is more than enough for you to get started. If you know this, you'll be able to talk to people in the silver market easily and you will learn what other things mean from them as you interact with them.

Here's your list:

3CN   U.S. Three Cent Nickel produced from 1865 to 1889.

ABT   About.

ACG   ACcu-Grade. Grading service. Controversial at present, because the assigned grades seem to be inflated relative to standard services like PCGS and NGC.

AG   About Good. Grade.

AGW   Actual Gold Weight

ANA   American Numismatic Association. Collector and dealer organization.

ANACS   (originally) American Numismatic Association Certification Service. Grading service. It has since been sold to a company independent of the ANA.

ASE   American Silver Eagle. A one-ounce silver bullion coin, issued 1986-date.

ASW   Actual Silver Weight

AT   Artificial Toning.

AU   About Uncirculated. Grade.

B# (B1-B10) Browning number (1925). Die variety - Bust Quarters, 1796-1838.
B# (B1-B23) Bolender number (1950, 1998). Die variety - Silver Dollars, 1794-1803.
BB# (BB1-BBn) Bowers and Borckardt number (1993). Die variety - Silver Dollars, 1794-1804 and later.
BG# Breen and Gillio number (1983). Die variety - California private gold, 1852-1882.
BIN Buy It Now.
BN Brown. Color grade for uncirculated copper coins (BN, RB, or RD).
BU Brilliant Uncirculated. Vague Grade.
BV Bullion Value. The value of the coin is closely related to its metallic content (usually silver or gold).
C# Cohen number (1982) for US Half Cents or Craig number for world coins
CMM# Cohen, Munson, Munde number
COA Certificate of Authenticity.
CSDG California Small Denomination Gold.
DC (DCAM) Deep Cameo. High grade proof.
DDO Doubled Die Obverse. Type of die variety.
DDR Doubled Die Reverse. Type of die variety.
DMPL Deep Mirror Proof Like. Business strike, with deep mirrored planchet.
EAC Early American Coppers, Inc. Collector and dealer organization.
EF (XF) Extra-Fine Grade.
F Fine Grade.
F.A.O. The Food and Agriculture Organization Coins were issued by member countries where a % of coin profits were given to the F.A.O.
FB Full Bands.
FBL Full Bell Lines.
FE Flying Eagle (cent).
FH Full Head.
FR# Robert Friedberg's numbering for world gold coins and British issues.
FS# (FS1-FS?) Fivaz and Stanton number
FS Full Steps.

FSB	Full Split Bands.
G	Good.
ICGS	Independent Coin Grading Service. Grading service.
IHC	Indian Head Cent. US cent coin.
J# (J1-J1778)	Judd number (1959-77). Pattern or experimental coin.
JR# (JR1-JR13)	John Reich number (Davis, et al, 1984). Die variety - Bust Dimes, 1794-1837.
KM# (KM1-KM)	Krause and Mishler number. From Standard Catalog of World Coins.
LM# (LM1-LM18)	Logan-McCloskey number (1998). Die variety - Bust Half Dimes, 1792-1837.
MM	Mint Mark
MS	Mint State. (Uncirculated, business strike). Grade.
N# (N1-N17)	Newcomb number (1944). Die variety - Large Cents, 1816-1868.
N# (N1-N105)	Newman number (1952). Die variety - Fugio Cents, 1787.
NGC	Numismatic Guarantee Corporation. Grading service.
NCLT	Non-Circulating Legal Tender
OGP	Original Government Packaging.
OMM	Over MintMark. Two different mintmarks involved. (versus **RPM**, which is the same mintmark punched more than once).
OMS	Off-Metal Strike
P#	Major Fred Pridmore's numbering for British colonial coinage.
PCGS	Professional Coin Grading Service. Grading service.
PCI	Photo-certified Coin Institute. Grading service.
PL	Proof Like. Business strike, with mirrored planchet.
PNG	Professional Numismatists Guild. Dealer organization.
PQ	Premium Quality. Sometimes part of the sealed slab grade, such as a MS64 PQ (not quite good enough for MS65). Often it is just a hype adjective like "Choice" or "Select".

PVC — Poly Vinyl Chloride. An ingredient of soft plastic "flip" coin holders which will damage coins over time.

R# (R1-R8) — Rarity scale. R1 most common; R8 least common.

RB — Red-Brown. Color grade for uncirculated copper coins (BN, RB, or RD).

RD — Red. Color grade for uncirculated copper coins (BN, RB, or RD).

RIC — Roman Imperial Coinage.

RNS — Royal Numismatic Society. Collector and dealer organization.

RPC — Roman Provincial Coinage.

RPD — RePunched Date. Type of die variety.

RPM — RePunched Mintmark. Type of die variety.

RSC — Roman Silver Coinage.

S# (S1-S295) — Sheldon number (1949). Die variety - Large Cents

S# (S1-S9) — Snow number (1992). Die variety - Flying Eagle and Indian Head Cents, 1856-1909.

SBA — Susan B. Anthony (dollar). US coin, 1979-1981,1999.

SEGS — Sovereign Entities Grading Service. Grading service.

SLQ — Standing Liberty Quarter. US coin, 1916-1930.

SMS — Special Mint Set

SP — Specimen. Better than business strike, but not quite a proof.

SQ — Statehood Quarters.

TPG — Third Party Grading

UC (UCAM) — Ultra Cameo. High grade proof.

UNC — Uncirculated. Grade.

VG — Very Good.Grade.

V# (V1-V10) — Valentine number

VAM# (VAM1-VAM230) — Van Allen and Mallis number

WL — Walking Liberty (half dollar). US coin, 1916-1947.

XF (EF) — Extra-Fine Grade.

Y# — R.S. Yeoman numbering for world coins.

YN — Young numismatic

www.ingramcontent.com/pod-product-compliance
Lightning Source LLC
Chambersburg PA
CBHW051242170526
45165CB00004B/1531